Delicious Conversations: Arriving At Unexpected Moments of Joy
© 2007 by Ruth M. Godfrey and Dawn Morningstar

Published by Gathering House
450 Emerald Lane
St. Paul, MN 55115

Ordering info: 612-735-1975
Visit us online at www.deliciousconversations.net

Cover design by Kathi Dunn, Dunn + Associates Design, www.dunn-design.com

Cover & interior illustrations by Jane Mjolsness, www.janemjolsness.com

Interior design by Liz Tufte, Folio Bookworks, www.folio-bookworks.com

Printed in the U.S.A.

ISBN-13: 978-0-9778269-8-8

We acknowledge the sacred process
that led to the manifestation of this book.

We affirmed the guidance of Spirit,
we listened, and then created.

Our heartfelt thanks to
Robert Hill and Carol Jean Johnson
and the many people who championed this idea
and believed in the value of this work.

table of contents

chapter 1

extend your invitation

You Are Invited

Picture this. You're late, hungry, and decide to pull into a fast-food restaurant. Quickly, you give the once-over to the menu on the sign, calculate in your head healthy food versus empty calories and order what you usually get anyway. After you recite your choice into the speaker box and are instructed to pull ahead to the first window, you pay, take your bag and begin to eat as you drive off.

Okay, maybe you avoid the fast food scene yet succumb to mindless eating from time to time. How does that make you feel?

Now, think about one of the best dining experiences you've ever enjoyed. Allow yourself to go there in your mind. Where were you? Who was there? What was the setting? How leisurely was your experience? How did the food feel in your mouth? How did your senses come alive? What made your experience extraordinary? How did you feel at the end of the meal?

When we recalled our own best dining experiences, some of the thoughts that came to mind included:

- Feeling welcome, special, nurtured, and cared for
- Experiencing a lovely atmosphere and presentation of food and setting
- Enjoying a well-planned meal, delicious and fresh, that ignited all of the senses
- Creating the possibilities for conversation, connectedness, and reflection
- Celebrating togetherness and being in the moment
- Expressing gratitude

What we discovered is that conversations can be as ordinary and pedestrian as eating fast food, or they can be as sublime and transcendent as your most cherished dining experience. In our hectic and complex world, we may miss the richness of each other's thoughts and feelings. We may miss each other's greatness.

Advancement of technology and the bombardment of choices in our culture can often lead us further and further apart — resulting in isolation, alienation, and loneliness. Human beings were created to be in deep relationship with one another. How can we be in soulful relationships, if we don't talk openly or listen deeply to the rhythm and core essence of each other's stories?

Delicious Conversations is an invitation for each of us to tell our story, and to reveal who we are to ourselves and to each other. Doing so leads us back to what has heart and meaning in our lives. This way of expression is a renaissance of rich relatedness that results in truly listening, sharing, and knowing one another.

Throughout this book, we have used the words *God* and *Spirit* and sometimes, *Universe*. May this serve to capture the essence of a higher power or unity that we believe enlivens and connects everything. The most important thing is that we all understand the intention for our inclusion of these names at all — which is quite simply, *Love*.

Bon Appetit!

Extend Your Invitation

Some of the words used to describe *delicious* are:

APPEALING	ENCHANTING	SCRUMPTUOUS
CHARMING	TASTY	LOVELY
DELIGHTFUL	LUSCIOUS	APPETIZING
PLEASANT	DELECTABLE	WONDERFUL

Imagine what your life would be like if all of your conversations were delicious. Well, they can be — any time, any place, and with anyone. As you experiment with the simple ideas in this book, you will find that it is an open invitation to create and experience deeper connection, and a sense of joy. Everyone — from your closest friend or family member, to a person you've just met or someone you may never see again — can be nourished and honored because of your awareness and practice of *Delicious Conversations* techniques. Your choice to engage with others in this way embraces our shared humanity and blesses us all.

chapter 2

select your menu

Select Your Menu

When choosing what to serve to your guests, recipes can inspire you how to prepare for your gathering and to select what ingredients you will need. Here are a few simple starter "recipes" to stir your imagination and whet your appetite for delicious conversations with anyone, anywhere.

For Your Recipe Collection

Set the Tone

1. Make eye contact

2. Minimize or disregard distractions

3. Be grateful

4. Create a sense of comfort

Be Present

1. Release anything that's keeping you from being present

2. Quiet your own internal dialogue

3. Maintain eye contact

4. Remain curious and engaged

Be Together

1. Pay attention to what has heart and meaning for the person who is sharing

2. Remain open to the full spectrum of emotions that may arise

3. Agree on what will be kept confidential

4. Release judgment and evaluation about what is being said — it is that person's reality just as yours is for you

Affirm and Celebrate

1. Bear witness to each other's greatness

2. Acknowledge what is being said

3. Let the person know with your facial expression and body language that you are hearing them

4. Celebrate what you hear

Answering the Questions:

1. Answer from your heart

2. Give voice to what's within you

3. Trust the person in front of you

4. Celebrate the deliciousness of your story

chapter 3

gather your ingredients

Your Ingredients

When raw ingredients are placed in a pot and cooked over a flame, they blend together and result in something very different than what was originally placed in the pot. Each item contributes to the wholeness of the dish and has the potential to alchemize into something delicious. When people come together in conversation, their ideas and unexpressed thoughts are like the raw ingredients. Stirred and simmered — questions, reflection, and sharing help us feel whole and complete.

In some cooking traditions, it is said that as ingredients are simmered together and allowed to sit for a bit, or even overnight in the refrigerator, the ultimate flavor is magnificently enhanced. It is said that the ingredients have "talked to each other." When people create the space and are open to truly genuine conversation, no matter how much time they have, they find new ways to talk to each other, as well.

Add Spice to Your Conversations

Ask the Questions

1. Choose an "Entrée" from Chapter 5

2. Ask the questions from that section

3. Come from a place of genuine curiosity

4. Ask your own empowering questions that begin with what, how, when, where or who. (Train yourself to refrain from using questions that begin with why. Why questions often lead to defensiveness and judgment which can cause the other person to shut down.)

Answer the Questions

1. Answer from your heart

2. Trust the person in front of you

3. Explore the answers that surface

4. Celebrate the deliciousness of what is said

Ask Deeper Questions

1. What more can you tell me about this?

2. What meaning does it have for you?

3. What choices are here for you?

4. What would you like to see happen?

Have Brave Conversations

1. Explore diverse perspectives to broaden understanding

2. Accept that uneasiness may occur

3. Express what you are feeling and be willing to move through it

4. Risk being vulnerable to arrive at a new level of intimacy

chapter 4

open your door

Open Your Door

Be Fully Present
      Listen Deeply
            Hear in a New Way
                  Trust What's Being Revealed

At the heart of any conversation is the desire to connect more deeply with another human being. Each wants to feel that they are being listened to, are being heard, and that their life stories are being witnessed. When we witness another's truth, *without judgment or evaluation*, we walk with them, acknowledging their unique value in the world. The person whose truth we are witnessing is able to explore how to be whole. Wholeness leads us to completeness and satisfaction, resulting in a deep sense of well being.

Conversation has the power to lead us to our wholeness when each person is fully present to the other. What does it mean to be fully present to what another is saying? It is to be still and to listen deeply. We quiet our mind and its racing thoughts, we set aside our desire to respond, we release our judgments and look intently into the eyes of the person speaking. A powerful message is given when we choose to be present in these ways. The message is "I care about you and what you are saying. I am open to connecting with your soul."

chapter 5

savor one another

Savor One Another

A simple reminder:

Create a sense of gratitude by starting
with a blessing or acknowledgment.

Take a moment to become quiet inside.

Share what's going on that might get in the
way of being present to a meaningful conversation.

Enjoy the greatness of the person in front of you.

A Blessing

We are grateful for questions asked
that stir our souls

and answers that bubble up
and delight us.

May all of our conversations
be delicious!

The Entrees

We are calling the next seven meaningful areas of our lives "entrees" because, on a menu, you choose what you would like to have. And here you can select what you'd like to focus on for your conversational centerpiece. Each "entrée" contains a thoughtful reflection, an opening observation, and seven questions in key areas of life that influence who we are and who we are becoming.

Use the questions from the "Entrees" section and then ask some of your own. It's been said that the best way to get a conversation going is to ask a person about him/herself. People *do* like to talk about themselves because it allows them to be heard and understood. Powerful questions, asked sincerely, peel away the layers that reveal what is in our hearts and help us to connect to one another in fresh, new ways.

Joy

Joy connects us to the deliciousness of the child within — igniting creativity, imagination and possibilities.

When we live with a sense of joy and delight, we are more aligned with what we've been called to this earth to do and be. Somewhere along the line, we get so caught up in the tediousness of everyday life that the childlike place within us seems to disappear. When that happens, life has a tendency to get heavy.

We are taught early in life to postpone or even silence our playfulness. Sit up straight, be quiet, don't laugh, only speak when you are spoken to, and you're being too silly are some of the commands that erode our spirit and diminish our capacity for creativity. New commands can be spoken that connect us to our creative self, where imagination lives and joy is ignited: slouch a little, be loud, belly-laugh, interrupt, or just be silly. Shifting the energy, changing direction, and being spontaneous or even outrageous are some of the ways to have fun and experience fullness of expression. We need to remember to acknowledge the joyful child within.

As we grow and evolve, so does our experience of joy. What we define as fun and play during earlier stages in our life may transcend into the richness of being. External situations may no longer feed us in the same way, yet we may be nourished by the simplicity of experiencing the present moment. How does this work? Openness to all that is — is all that is required. Savoring the beauty of standing on top of a mountain may replace the thrill of skiing down it. When and how joy arrives varies from person to person. Joy comes as a delightful surprise beckoning one to be in awe of what is.

1. What is the difference between joy and happiness?

2. When was the first time you experienced joy in your life? What do you remember about it?

3. How is joy connected to your experience of peace?

4. What do you love doing so much that time seems to disappear when you are doing it?

5. Tell an imaginary story about you living a day filled with joy.

6. How does joy ignite your passion for living?

7. What is a new way you could access more joy in your life?

Spirituality

Spirituality reveals God as each of us.

Ask people about their spirituality and you are likely to get a variety of descriptions of beliefs. Some would answer that their spirituality is their religion, faith, or dogma. Others may say that their intuition is their link to Spirit or being in nature helps them sense the sacred. Some may answer "I'm not spiritual at all."

The dictionary defines spirituality as "having the nature of spirit." If that is the case, then *everything* is spiritual and *everyone* is a spiritual being because everything is of Spirit. The fact that there is something else, something greater, is an inherent truth that even scientists are uncovering. As they explore smaller and smaller units of matter, they are discovering there is always something underneath. Could that "something underneath" be God?

Knowing and acknowledging that God is the basic building block of all that is, gives us a view of life that embraces the sacred. As we embrace the sacred, life takes on greater meaning and purpose. Living with a sense of reverence for everything that is gives us faith to trust that everything is happening just as it is meant to be. Choosing to trust allows us to live whole and authentic in God's image and likeness.

1. How would you describe your spirituality?

2. What does it take to walk your spiritual path?

3. What do you view as sacred?

4. Tell a story of a time when you felt whole and authentic.

5. What would your life be like if you believed that everything is part of a Divine plan?

6. When do you experience reverence?

7. How has your understanding of faith influenced who you are and how you are in the world?

43

High Dream

*Living our high dream is our greatest gift
to humanity and to ourselves.*

We come to this earth to live out our high dream. Some people may call their high dream their life purpose; others call it their reason for being or their promise for the world. However we define it, our high dream is our most sacred assignment here on earth. It is what we have come here to do, to say, and to be. How this high dream is chosen is unclear. Are we the ones who choose our high dream, does God assign it to us, or is it co-created? What is clear is that when we uncover our high dream and then live it fully, our lives are blessed. When we don't honor our gift, we may feel fragmented, alienated and empty. We are always at choice as to how we will express our high dream.

How will you know what your high dream is? Perhaps the very first thing to do is to examine your own questions about life and living. What makes you feel the most alive and awake in the world? What ignites your passion? When do you feel that your contributions matter? The answers to these questions and others will lead you to your high dream. Keep asking the questions.

Finding your way to your high dream is an exploration and a journey that unfolds throughout your life. The essence of your high dream remains unchanged, yet who you are being allows you to add dimensions to the expression of your high dream. Living the high dream is the calling of your soul to manifest the Divine here on earth. As lofty as that sounds, it is the most authentic way you can live and has the greatest potential for grace to show up in your life.

1. What is it that you have secretly wanted to do, be, or create?

2. What connection do you see between your secret wish and your high dream (life purpose)?

3. What is your high dream?

4. How does living your high dream connect you with your sacred self?

5. How is your life today an active expression of your high dream?

6. How could you attract others to your high dream?

7. When you live your high dream, what difference does it make in the world?

Surroundings

*The beauty and peace we embrace satisfies
our hunger for inspiration and feeds our souls.*

When we think of surroundings, we are really talking about wherever we physically are in the moment: our home, nature, our office, our yard or any other place we may find ourselves. There is a profound connectedness between us and where we are. Surroundings can inspire us, lower our energy or affect us in a whole spectrum of ways in between. In any case, our surroundings can change us. We have the power to transform our environment and are always at choice—we can influence our surroundings or be affected by them. (And sometimes, it is a little of both.)

Beauty is inherent in nature and gives us clues on how to shape our own experience in relation to our environment. Many people say that they feel best when they are out in nature. What is it about the gifts found in our natural environment that call to us and how can we listen and respond? Once we've heard the call, how can we take the elements found in nature that have meaning for us and mix them into our environment?

Peace and beauty seem to be some of the necessary ingredients for any recipe that creates surroundings that nurture. Candles, plants, flowers, fountains, essential oils, color, and a sense of order are things we can use outside of ourselves to create beauty. Centering ourselves, using deep breathing, being still and living in the present moment are some of the internal methods we can use to restore our inner peace. The beauty and peace that we foster and send out into the world has the potential to inspire and fulfill everyone it touches. When we experience beauty and peace in our lives, it satisfies our hunger for inspiration and feeds our souls.

1. How do your surroundings move you?

2. What do you love about your surroundings?

3. What are the ingredients for creating surroundings that nurture you?

4. What changes would transform an environment in your life?

5. What meaningful themes from places you have lived still influence what you want today?

6. How do your surroundings say who you are to the world?

7. How are your surroundings an expression of your soul?

50

Balance

*Living a life of balance leads us to
find the middle way,
savoring each moment
as the gift that it is.*

Many people believe that it would be really easy to live a life of balance
and peaceful harmony "if only" they were monks or holy people — spend-
ing their days in quiet prayer and meditation, rather than worrying
about the everydayness of life. Perhaps this is true, yet there is a richness that exists *because* of all that life brings us. The choice is to embrace
rather than push away what life presents us — seeing it for the gift that it
is. Choosing to live like this becomes our balance pole (like the one used
by high wire performers) to find the middle way.

What does it mean to find the middle way? It means not getting caught
up in a tangle of drama, but consciously choosing to walk *through* life
(rather than pushing it away), and allowing ourselves to see all sides of
any matter. In doing so, we make greater choices and pave the way for
living with a sense of peace.

Once we find the middle way and walk it, we live positioned in the center
of our lives. This gives us a panoramic view from the center that allows
us to see all that is possible. This leads us to an authentic experience of
balance rather than one that is limited and capable of being thrown
off at any moment. The old paradigm of balance seems to be influenced
by external forces rather than a purposeful internal response. It takes
awareness, practice, and tenacity to live the middle way.

1. What brings balance into your life?

2. When you reflect on balance in your life, what do you discover?

3. What sustains balance in your life?

4. What one action could you take to have more balance in your life?

5. Tell a story about a time when you were living in balance and harmony.

6. How does living in balance expand your life?

7. What are you willing to do to live a life of balance?

55

Abundance

*Abundance is the freedom
to live in full measure.*

When we think of nature, it is constantly renewing itself — always abundant in its re-creation. Nature reflects a deep trust that all is provided and participates in the active and constant flow of life. Abundance flows through our lives as well, when we are active participants in the feast of life. Abundance is always present, seen or unseen. It is up to us to recognize it and enjoy it to the fullest.

Abundance wears many faces. It shows up as health, energy, relationships, vocation, money, lifestyle, surroundings, faith, and our freedom to live fully. When one of these areas in our life seems not to be in abundance (flowing), we may tend to focus so much on what's not working, that we begin to believe that NOTHING is working. What we focus on the most expands — abundance or famine. The choice is ours.

In the area of money, some people may say, "I don't see how I could be responsible for changing the flow of abundance in my life. I go to work, get my paycheck, pay my bills, and then the money is gone." Attraction begins with the words we choose to describe our situation and is furthered by a shift in how we see things. Going back to the statement above, a different way to say it might be, "I am open to abundance in my life, by affirming its active and constant flow. I am grateful for the work I have and the money that I have attracted. I now invite more money into my life and am open to receiving it." This same change of mind and words can be used in other areas of life as well, and gives us the freedom to experience the fullness of who we have come to be.

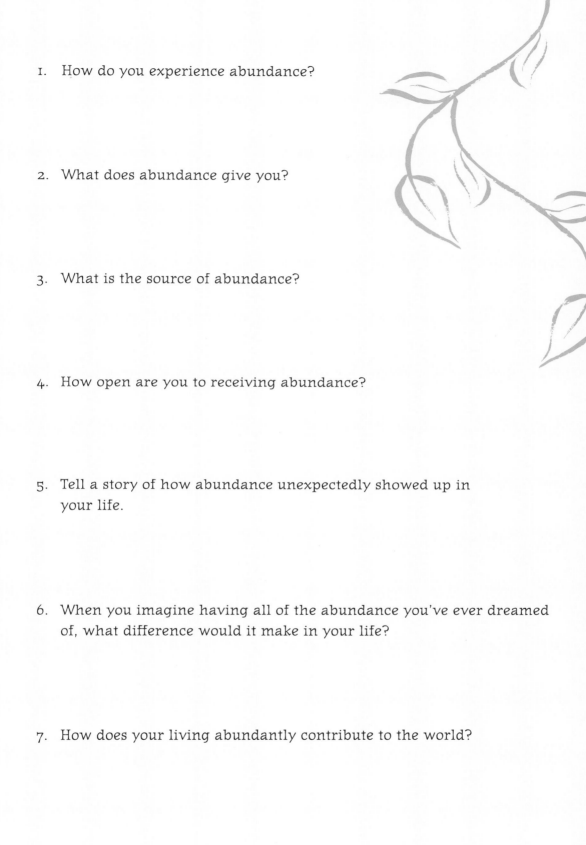

1. How do you experience abundance?

2. What does abundance give you?

3. What is the source of abundance?

4. How open are you to receiving abundance?

5. Tell a story of how abundance unexpectedly showed up in your life.

6. When you imagine having all of the abundance you've ever dreamed of, what difference would it make in your life?

7. How does your living abundantly contribute to the world?

Relationships

*Relationships exist
to reveal our wholeness.*

Relationships are another reason we have come to earth. They allow us to love and to be open to receiving love. Relationships are the keys to the mystery of uncovering our own wholeness. Think of Tom Hanks in the movie, *Castaway*, where he finds himself totally alone on a deserted island. After fulfilling his basic need for food, water and shelter, he could no longer go on until he created the vessel for a relationship – Wilson, the soccer ball. Was it a real relationship or a fantasy? It doesn't matter, because it allowed him the potential for love. In the scene when the castaway throws Wilson overboard, suddenly he experiences a deep sense of loss. In retrieving Wilson, he felt whole again.

There may be times when we want to throw relationships overboard because they feel hard, old, destructive, or inauthentic. Even when we discard our relationships, the truth is we never really end them because they are woven together for all eternity. Relationships that have "ended" have simply changed form. A marriage that ends does not erase the connection that existed. Friendships that have run their course may leave us with unanswered questions. In our search for answers and meaning inspired by being in relationship, we see another part of who we are – more whole and complete than we could be on our own. We cannot do this alone.

We are as changed by relationships as we will allow ourselves to be. We may not always know or understand the lessons each relationship brings into our lives, yet there is a purpose to each. Wisdom invites us to discover what the lessons may be. We become more whole as we integrate the lessons into our lives that have been gifted to us.

We attract people into our lives to help us uncover our potential for greatness. Some relationships are easy and their gift is obvious, while other gifts we receive from the people in our lives are masked. When we examine and then trust the relationships we have in our lives at the moment, lessons are more likely to be revealed.

Relationships begin before we are born, continue throughout our lives, and extend beyond our time on earth. Each relationship serves up another piece of who we are and who we are becoming. We are always related because we are one.

1. What do relationships reveal about who you are?

2. What is delicious about relationships?

3. What do you want more of in your relationships?

4. Tell a story of a time you felt whole and complete in a relationship.

5. What have you learned from a relationship that has ended?

6. How does your relationship with yourself influence your relationship with others?

7. What relationships have unexpectedly transformed you?

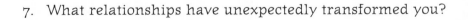

World View

When we experience the world as a possibility our lives overflow with possibility.

In thinking about the world, we are able to choose how we see it. We can choose to see it from the perspective of what's wrong and sad, or what's right and possible. When we see the world fully, we are free to be an expression of love's creation. We cannot love and judge at the same time. There's no room for both. There is plenty of room, however, for love's companion — compassion. Compassion is defined as the Latin *com* (with) and the Latin *pati* (to suffer). A more evolved meaning could be *to come with passion.*

What does coming to the world with passion mean? It means living with reverence, acceptance, and being fully committed. All becomes sacred to us. Yes, all. It is a huge leap, to have the faith that there is a master plan at work in the universe (and perhaps beyond). Everything is occurring precisely as it is should in this moment. We may not always be privy to the why of what is, yet at times we may receive clues that expand the sacredness of our lives and reveal what needs to change. Being fully awake allows us to receive the gift of what is there and what is missing. Forgiveness and love are the essential ingredients for waking from the dream of our collective illusion of what we believe the world is and is not. Once we awaken from our illusion, we are beckoned to take a stand and do the work that we are called to do.

The world is the sacred container for humanity and inside the world, relationships and *experiences* occur. When judgment and a sense of separateness show up, they create a veil of illusion in the world that blocks us from seeing what is possible. Being willing to *experience* the power of relationships in the world removes the veil of illusion and opens the way to understanding who and what we really are and what we came to do.

We have come to experience our holy relationship with God (or a greater power), each other, and ourselves. The world is our perfect experiment to remember our wholeness. When we experience wholeness within ourselves, we feel on track, connected, and live life with passion. When the world experiences wholeness, humanity evolves and has the power to heal, thrive, and continue.

1. What do you love about living at this time?

2. What adventure would you like to experience in the world?

3. What illusions keep you separate from the world?

4. Tell a story of living in a perfect world.

5. What do you hold sacred in the world?

6. How could you connect with humanity in a bold, new way?

7. What legacy are you creating for humankind?

chapter 6

wish each other well

Wish Each Other Well

Thank you for having this delicious conversation with us. Using our metaphor, the meal is over and no one wants to leave. Aromas remain in the air, bearing witness to a well savored repast. Full and satisfied, there is an inner knowing that you have experienced the deliciousness of deep and sentient conversation.

Things that make it easier to say goodbye: acknowledge everyone who made the experience possible, celebrate how your soul was fed, and be an emissary of the practice of delicious conversation whenever you can.

The practice of delicious conversation creates movement in the world because it brings people together in a purposeful way. Just as food is essential to our existence, so is connection to one another.

The words in this book and the thoughts in your mind intermingle to create a fresh new recipe for rich relatedness. May all of your conversations be delicious!

chapter 7

your reflections & notes

Reflections on Your Delicious Gatherings

The following pages are reserved for you to create a legacy of memorable gatherings. Envision one hundred years from today someone discovers this recording of gatherings that you have preserved. What difference will it make to the one who finds it? What will it tell them about what was sacred to you and the people in your life? How will what you wrote inspire them to have delicious conversations with the people in their lives?

Each reflection page also includes space for affixing a photo, memento, a drawing, or anything that is symbolic of your gatherings. Whatever you decide to do with your pages is perfect — a few words, visuals, or even doodles have the power to capture the magic.

The date of our gathering:

Those who shared time together:

How we connected — what we ate and drank:

Memories we'll treasure:

The date of our gathering:

Those who shared time together:

How we connected — what we ate and drank:

Memories we'll treasure:

The date of our gathering:

Those who shared time together:

How we connected — what we ate and drank:

Memories we'll treasure:

The date of our gathering:

Those who shared time together:

How we connected — what we ate and drank:

Memories we'll treasure:

The date of our gathering:

Those who shared time together:

How we connected — what we ate and drank:

Memories we'll treasure:

85

The date of our gathering:

Those who shared time together:

How we connected — what we ate and drank:

Memories we'll treasure:

The date of our gathering:

Those who shared time together:

How we connected — what we ate and drank:

Memories we'll treasure:

The date of our gathering:

Those who shared time together:

How we connected — what we ate and drank:

Memories we'll treasure:

The date of our gathering:

Those who shared time together:

How we connected — what we ate and drank:

Memories we'll treasure:

The date of our gathering:

Those who shared time together:

How we connected — what we ate and drank:

Memories we'll treasure:

The date of our gathering:

_____

Those who shared time together:

_____

_____

_____

_____

_____

How we connected — what we ate and drank:

_____

_____

_____

_____

_____

Memories we'll treasure:

_____

_____

_____

The date of our gathering:

_____

Those who shared time together:

_____

_____

_____

_____

_____

How we connected — what we ate and drank:

_____

_____

_____

_____

_____

Memories we'll treasure:

_____

_____

_____

_____

The date of our gathering:

Those who shared time together:

How we connected — what we ate and drank:

Memories we'll treasure:

The date of our gathering:

Those who shared time together:

How we connected — what we ate and drank:

Memories we'll treasure:

The date of our gathering:

Those who shared time together:

How we connected — what we ate and drank:

Memories we'll treasure:

The date of our gathering:

Those who shared time together:

How we connected — what we ate and drank:

Memories we'll treasure:

The date of our gathering:

Those who shared time together:

How we connected — what we ate and drank:

Memories we'll treasure:

The date of our gathering:

Those who shared time together:

How we connected – what we ate and drank:

Memories we'll treasure:

The date of our gathering:

Those who shared time together:

How we connected — what we ate and drank:

Memories we'll treasure:

The date of our gathering:

Those who shared time together:

How we connected — what we ate and drank:

Memories we'll treasure:

The date of our gathering:

Those who shared time together:

How we connected — what we ate and drank:

Memories we'll treasure:

The date of our gathering:

Those who shared time together:

How we connected — what we ate and drank:

Memories we'll treasure:

The date of our gathering:

Those who shared time together:

How we connected — what we ate and drank:

Memories we'll treasure:

121

The date of our gathering:

Those who shared time together:

How we connected — what we ate and drank:

Memories we'll treasure:

About the Authors

Ruth M. Godfrey is a Master Life Coach and a trailblazer in revolutionary coaching technologies. She is President of Learning Journeys International Center of Coaching.

Dawn Morningstar is the co-host of the "Delicious Conversations" radio show, an inspirational speaker, and Master Life Coach in private practice.

Both Ruth and Dawn are committed to "soulful relationships that call us to experience love."

Our Wish for the World

All people have delicious conversations
resulting in a new way of understanding,
celebrating, and experiencing
unexpected moments of joy.

Gathering House

Gathering House coaches authors, publishes books and other print materials, and promotes inspirational gatherings globally. It is a forum for ideas and ways that inspire delicious living, reveal inner wisdom and champion each person to live their high dream.

You are invited to visit our websites at

www.deliciousconversations.net

and

www.learningjourneys.net